Making Sense
of 21st Century
Health Insurance Plans

▶ **A Fresh Look At Upfront Deductibles, FSAs, HRAs & HSAs**

Jonathan Pierpont Warner, *CEBS, ISCEBS Fellow*

1st Printing April 2009
Publisher Record Number: 1497874
ISBN: 978-0-692-00320-6

Printed by
Brilliant Graphics
400 Eagleview Boulevard
Exton, PA 19341
Printed in the United States of America

Limit of Liability / Disclaimer of Warranty: Great effort has been taken
to prepare this book and the educational material provided herein. At
the same time its contents may not fit all readers and individuals, and
thus its makes no representations, warranties or implied warranties
as to its fitness for a particular situation. The author shall not be liable
for any damages, whether special, incidental or consequential incurred
that result from information contained in this book or the external and
online resources it references.

This book has been crafted to be educational, with sufficient technical
information to act as a reference guide. It includes stories about
individuals and families to provide rationale for the efficient purchase
of important health insurance protection. The characters in the text
and their circumstances are fictional. Similarities to actual persons or
families are purely coincidental.

Dedicated to:
The Health and Welfare of
The American People

FORWARD

My first encounter with Jonathan Warner was almost 40 years ago. I was a wrestler and recent graduate from Lehigh University, and an insurance colleague of his father Cameron. Like it was yesterday, I remember grappling on the living room floors with the kids of my friends, and especially enjoyed tossing around the three Warner boys in their Lehigh Valley, Pennsylvania home. Although he never took up the sport, in this tome Jonathan, in a cerebral way, successfully wrestles us through proven, contemporary opportunities to maintain value while reducing personal and employer health care expenditures.

Jonathan Warner was virtually born into the insurance industry. His dad owned a highly successful insurance agency. He joined his father's firm after college, and sought my counsel at times as his career matured.

Jon was properly seasoned for an entrepreneurial career following his graduation from Middlebury College and early work with Massachusetts Mutual. Stints at the Johnson Companies and EBP HealthPlans / First Health, helped him develop an expertise assisting larger employer groups with managing health and welfare benefits. Brother Andrew and he continue today counseling employers and individuals with insurance and investment needs.

After founding JP Warner Associates, Inc. in 1997, he anticipated the popularity of Consumer Driven Health Plans, acquiring the third party administrator (TPA) Human Resource Administrators, Inc. in 2003. With Andrew and Warner Benefits, Inc., the brothers Warner successfully partner in a manner that helps all the businesses flourish. Their reputation as experts is well established in the Mid-Atlantic region of our great country.

Prior to this book, Jon published an article in the 1980's on HMO legislation changes, and "From Managed Care to Financed Care" in 2002, which has been on the syllabus at the Dartmouth College Tuck School of Business.

Jon strives to be an industry scholar. His organizational skills, combined with an ability to foresee the future of health care delivery, has been recognized by providers of health care, insurers, brokers, and clients. With all of the volumes of accomplishments on Jon's "page," his most impressive attribute might be his willingness to partner with others. Jon is a true "team player," whether it is in health care, a local non-profit board, or the school activities of his children. Although his business activities keep him busy, the seemingly tireless author has always found time for his wife, daughters and son. Community, church, and volunteerism are high priorities.

With the future of healthcare in America on the verge of revolutionary change, the words and thoughts of this "expert" are very timely. I expect that what follows will enlighten the minds of American citizens, industry leaders, employers, entrepreneurs, and politicians.

Michael J. Caruso, CLU, ChFC   March, 2009

"All truth goes through three stages.
First it is ridiculed.
Second it is strongly opposed.
Third it becomes self evident."

19th Century Philosopher
Arthur Schopenhauer

CONTENTS

SECTION ONE - ALIGNING PERSPECTIVES

SECTION TWO – RISK VS. COVERAGE

SECTION THREE – THE BIG PICTURE

SECTION ONE
Aligning Perspectives

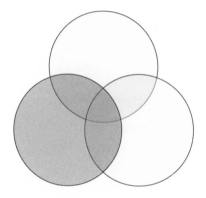

I. The Beginning

Health care and health insurance in America are expensive. Many citizens are over-insured, under-insured or totally lacking in health insurance protection. Health plans offered to Americans reflect a history of coverage expectations supported by government legislation. Analyses prove that individuals with 100% health insurance coverage, or low out-of-pocket copayment plans consume over time, an excessive amount of health care.

On the other hand, the under-insured are financially exposed to catastrophic and chronic health care costs, because low-cost coverage plans include dollar limits and pre-existing condition exclusions. People who lack insurance and receive health care services pay too much for care, because their cost is based on a Charge Master, often double or triple the discounted fee negotiated by insurance companies and government plans.

The history of the United States private and public health insurance system began in the early 20th century with our hospitals. To enhance their value and stabilize revenue, they banded together in the

1930's to form Hospital Service Plans. Using the concept of insurance, a small premium was paid by individuals, guaranteeing them inpatient care as needed. By spreading the cost of care to a large group, individual citizens paid little to cover the cost of the few whose health care needs required significant treatment.

Hospital Insurance Plans, which eventually became the national network of regional insurers known as Blue Cross, took time to catch on, receiving an enrollment boost in the 1940's as employers agreed to pay premiums for workers to enhance compensation during a period of war time wage and price controls. Tax deductible employer paid hospitalization insurance premiums became an accepted cost of doing business.

In the 1950's as people sought more physician care, Blue Shield plans emerged, introducing allowing the cost of the doctor's in-patient services to remain affordable. By design, Blue Cross and Blue Shield plans paid 100% of the cost of care, up to certain limits. There were a limited number of services available and many of the health conditions and cures we know today had not been isolated for treatment.

Insurance coverage for office visits and prescriptions eventually became available with the addition of Major Medical insurance. Even though hospitalization expenses and the cost of a physician's services in the hospital were paid in full by health insurance plans, Major Medical coverage required satisfaction of a deductible, and then payment of 20% of the cost of care. This established a basis for cost sharing to keep premiums low.

Major Medical plans were originally marketed by for-profit insurers. These companies developed comprehensive health insurance products and competed for employer business with the regional Blue Cross and Blue Shield plans. Their national administrative reach often better served multi-site employers.

Health care legislation's first great impact on our citizenry began with Medicare in the 1960's, followed by the HMO Act in 1973. The social and financial affects of these laws is still evolving. An interesting difference between them is that Medicare includes cost sharing with deductibles and coinsurance. HMOs generally charge flat copayments per visit. The Medicare Part A deductible changes each year with our cost of living. In 2009, the Part A deductible reached $1,068. Part B includes a $135 deductible and then requires 20% coinsurance, with no out of pocket maximum.

The HMO Act of 1973 promulgated a pre-payment system to physicians for basic health care needs, eliminating deductibles and coinsurance for workers in favor of flat copayments. HMO plans include preventive care services to promote good health, counter to traditional "sick insurance" plans. They established contractual relationships with hospitals and doctors to share risk in the treatment of patients.

Copayment plans formed the basis of the late 20th Century era know as the Managed Care period. HMOs (Health Maintenance Organizations), PPOs (Preferred Provider Organizations and POS (Point of Service) plans dominated. Pre-payment contracts with providers of care minimized premium increases and out-of-pocket responsibility.

With an aging population and ever increasing number of available and state mandated health care services, premium rate escalation prompted employers to charge employees higher amounts out of their paychecks for health coverage. Too many small employers stopped offering health insurance to workers because of cost.

The doubling of premiums in the first decade of the 21st century has prompted new thinking about how much pre-paid health coverage we should purchase. In 2002, rules were released allowing employers to offer a Health Reimbursement Arrangement (HRA). Employers use HRAs to reimburse, on a tax deductible basis, qualified health care expenses covered, but not paid by an insurance plan. Legislation signed at the end of 2003 introducing prescription coverage for seniors also created Health Savings Accounts (HSA). These pre-tax savings plans are similar to an Individual Retirement Account (IRA), eligible only to participants in a qualified High Deductible Health Plan (HDHP).

Flexible Spending Accounts (FSA), first enacted in 1978 to allow the pre-tax payment of qualified health expenses, were enhanced in 2005 and 2006 with the addition of Over-The-Counter (OTC) products and therapies available for reimbursement on a pre-tax basis. A 2 ½ month extension to use up FSA deferrals lessened concerns about the "Use it or Lose it Rule," increasing the popularity of these voluntary health care plans.

Employers who have embraced HSAs, HRAs and FSAs are flattening health care costs for their employees and businesses. And yet, since it is such a different approach than what many are used to, acceptance, even though logical, has been slow. FSAs, HRAs and HSAs are detailed in Chapter X.

Health Plan Design Continuum

1930's	1973	1980's	1990's	2002	2004
Traditional Indemnity *Insurance*	**HMO** *Coverage*	**PPO** *Coverage*	**POS** *Coverage*	Consumer Driven Health Plan (HRA) *Coverage & Insurance*	High Deductible Health Plan (HSA) *Insurance*

II. Comparing Health Insurance Options
Ann's Opportunity

For Ann, it ultimately became her best investment of the year. Some of her co-workers made out even better. Growing up, Ann's mother Helen worked two days a week in an insurance office. She was in a great mood and made the tastiest meals after a day resolving claims issues for people. Ann did not know what it was about insurance that intrigued her Mom, but she always said "You should pay for good insurance, because you never know when you will need it." Ann, like most of us, assumed the more expensive the plan the better. She initially wondered why her employer was now promoting:

A. A new plan option with low payroll contributions and upfront deductibles
B. The importance of 100% catastrophic protection
C. An FSA pre-tax account to cover qualified health expenses not paid by insurance

When Ann went online to view her Open-Enrollment plan options, she was intrigued by a new plan being offered by her employer. The payroll deductions were low. This interested her because she and her fiancé were trying to save money for a down payment on a new home. She then looked at the coverage details and at first felt deflated. Before the plan paid anything, she had to satisfy a $2,000 deductible! The deductible applied to hospital stays, surgery, lab work, x-rays, office visits and even prescriptions. The only service covered in full (after a $20 copay) was an annual preventive care visit.

Then she noticed that her employer was offering to reimburse the first $1,000 of the deductible. It sounded interesting, but she was not certain that the risk was worth it. And, she had been raised to believe you always pay for good insurance, because you never know when you will need it.

The following day Ann brought up the new high deductible option during a visit at Helen's long term care facility. Even though Ann's mother had retired a few years back and lost the use of her legs, her mind was quite sharp. She normally read two newspapers a day plus a weekly business magazine. She especially enjoyed the articles about insurance.

After describing the new plan option, Helen posed these questions to Ann:

A. How much will you save next year in payroll deductions for the high deductible plan?
B. Can you estimate how much you will spend in copays this year for medical care?
C. Does your company offer a Flexible Spending Account?
D. Is the $1,000 paid by your employer available through a Health Reimbursement Arrangement (HRA) or a Health Savings Account (HSA)?
E. Is the coverage 100% after the deductible is satisfied?

Ann struggled to find all of the answers online. She knew that her mother would be disappointed if she did not have the details by the time of her next visit. Finally she noticed the Q&A section, and confirmed the answers by sending an email to her employer's human resources group.

First Ann compared her current plan's cost of $50 per bi-weekly pay to the high deductible plan at $25 per pay. Her pay would increase $650 per year if she chose the high deductible plan. Next she looked at copays this year for medical care, and figured out that four office visits cost $120, an x-ray of her wrist after slipping on the ice cost $60, and her two prescriptions cost $60 every three months through mail order. In total, she spent $400 out-of-pocket the current year.

She then found out that her employer offers a voluntary Flexible Spending Account (FSA) plan that allows pre-tax payment of out-of-pocket health expenses. She also learned that the $1,000 from her employer was available either through a HRA or an HSA.

Her mother's final question involved the coverage after the deductible. Ann printed the plan summaries to compare both options and felt good about being prepared to discuss the answers.

During their next visit, Helen's first question kind of surprised her, and made her chuckle inside. Her Mom asked whether Ann had already decided on the plan to select. "Why would I do that before seeking your advice, Mom" she said. "Because you usually already have your mind made up by the time you come to me."

"Well, I like the fact that I can reduce medical plan payroll deductions and increase my take home pay, plus I save on copays because the first half of the deductible is 100% reimbursed. It looks like I might save $1,000 or more next year. But I must be missing something; isn't this too good to be true?"

Helen asked to see the plan summaries and clarified that in the new plan, once the deductible has been satisfied in-network, the coverage is 100% for hospitalization, laboratory tests, emergency visits and doctor's office visits.

"Did you know that if you had to go into the hospital for a couple of nights, your current plan requires you to spend $500 in copays? In fact, you are at risk for up to $1,250 if you are an inpatient for five nights or more. Also, it doesn't indicate that there is an overall maximum out-of-pocket for copays. This is very interesting and makes the new plan seem simple in comparison."

"It is appealing, the more that I study this Upfront Deductible Plan. It reminds me of the Major Medical policies that were popular when you were born. Your current copay plan 'nickels and dimes' you every time you receive or purchase health

Chart B - Upfront Deductible Plan	In NETWORK	Out of NETWORK
	Health Reimbursement	
Benefits and Services	**$1,000 SINGLE / $2,000 FAMILY**	
Annual Deductible		
Individual	$2,000	$5,000
Family	$4,000	$10,000
After Deductible Plan Pays	100%	50%
Coinsurance limit		
Individual	$5,600	$10,000
Family	$11,200	$20,000
Lifetime Maximum	Unlimited	$500,000
Routine Mammography	100%, no Deductible	50%
Child immunizations	100%, no Deductible	50%
Routine Physical	$20 Copay 100%	50%
Routine GYN Exam	$20 Copay 100%	50%
Well Child Care	$20 Copay 100%	50%
Emergency Room	After Deductible, 100%	50%
Physician Office	After Deductible, 100%	50%
Specialist Office	After Deductible, 100%	50%
Chiropractic	After Deductible, 100%	50%
Inpatient Hospital	After Deductible, 100%	50%
Outpatient Hospital	After Deductible, 100%	50%
Maternity	After Deductible, 100%	50%
Surgery and Anesthesia	After Deductible, 100%	50%
Lab / X-Ray	After Deductible, 100%	50%
Physical Therapy	After Deductible, 100%	50%
Inpatient Psychiatric	After Deductible, 100%	50%
Outpatient Psychiatric	After Deductible, 100%	50%
Prescription Drugs	_After Deductible is Satisfied_	
Retail Rx	$10 Generic / $30 Preferred / $50 NP	
Mail Order Rx	$20 Generic / $60 Preferred / $100 NP	

care services. Sure you take some risk with the $1,000 cost responsibility, and I see you must pay copays for prescriptions after the deductible is satisfied, but all hospitalization and surgery expenses are 100% covered after the deductible. I'm surprised they call it a High Deductible Health Plan, since when you compound inflation, the purchasing power of $1,000 is equal to $100 just twenty-five years ago!"

Ann informed Helen that she could receive the entire HRA $1,000 immediately as needed. The FSA allowed her to reduce her pay to cover the second $1,000 of the deductible on a pre-tax basis. She would not put that much away because of the Use it Or Lose It rule, but appreciated knowing the option existed for future years. Helen's insurance knowledge kicked in as she scribbled the following comparison.

Chart C – Ann's Financial Analysis

Current Plan:	$1,300 in payroll deductions
	$ 420 in expected copays
	$1,720 KNOWN COST
Additional risk:	$1,250 if hospitalized
Total	**$2,970**

New Plan:	$650 in payroll deductions
	<u>$0 in expected copays</u>
	$650 KNOWN COST
Additional risk:	$1,000 if hospitalized
Total	**$1,650**

Potential savings: $1,070 - $1,320

"So have you made up your mind now?" Helen asked. "I have Mom, including taking the HRA versus the HSA. The entire $1,000 is available in January. The same is true for what I put into the FSA. The HSA funds will be deposited each pay throughout the year. This means that by the end of January, unless I add more, there will be less than $100 available to reimburse my deductible. Some day I think I will want an HSA, but now protecting my cash flow and saving to buy a house are more important."

III. An Extra Step Made Easier with A Debit Card

Of course there are always more details when it comes to health insurance plans. What follows may induce "detail fatigue" for some, and inspire others.

By choosing the new plan, Ann was agreeing to invest more time to manage her health care. Even though her employer covered the first half of the deductible, she accepted responsibility to make certain the bills got paid. Ann understood that as long as she used in-network doctors and hospitals, payment was at the discounted price. In order to have access to the HRA funds, the plan required her to be treated in network.

The purchase of prescriptions seemed straightforward. When visiting a pharmacy or mailing away for prescriptions, she had to provide her health insurance card along with a health-care-only, or limited use MasterCard® debit card. Prescriptions, instantly discounted at the time of purchase, were finalized by swiping the card and pressing the "charge" button on the machine. This at first seemed odd since she was issued a "debit" card, and there is a button on the machine marked for debit purchases.

The explanation is that health care only debit cards are "PIN-less." One presses the "charge" button if no PIN (Personal Identification Number) is required. The Master-Card is a "limited use, category code restricted" card that will not work to purchase gasoline or pay for groceries.

Purchasing a prescription is straightforward, while hospital and doctor visit payments add time to the cycle. At the conclusion of a visit, the office staff checks your insurance card or an online system to confirm coverage, and you are on your way. Since the entire discounted cost of the visit is covered subject to the satisfaction of the Upfront Deductible, payment is made after the claim is processed by the insurance company.

The office staff bills the insurance company, listing their "charge." The insurer discounts the charge and mails an EOB (Explanation of Benefits) to the billing office and the patient's home. The EOB lists the charge amount and the discounted, covered amount that is due.

The invoice is mailed to the patient, who is responsible for paying the discounted amount. The patient fills in the numbers from their debit card on the invoice and mails it back, allowing automatic payment from the HRA.

This all seems simple, but it is possible this efficient system will break down.

1. What if the office staff demands a copayment upfront?
2. What if the provider office does not accept debit card payments?
3. What if the HRA administrator requires "substantiation" back up to confirm the debit card was used for proper purchases?
4. What happens if Ann runs out of HRA funds on her debit card?

If the office staff demands a copayment, agree to a $20 swipe from your debit card and be certain this shows up as a credit when invoiced.

If the provider does not accept debit card payments, the patient should make payment with cash or check and request payment from the administrator.

The administrator may demand substantiation of a debit card payment. By scan and email, or fax of an EOB, validation of the service is confirmed. These medical debit cards will not work to purchase gas for your auto. The IRS has high standards for ensuring a health care purchase is a qualified expense.

Funds available on the debit card may be exhausted before one's out-of-pocket responsibility is satisfied. In this situation, personal after tax payment responsibility is necessary until the deductible is satisfied in full. Deferring enough money into an FSA eliminates this inconvenience and reduces taxes. A health care debit card should be smart enough to know whether a service is HRA and/or FSA eligible.

Companies are developing payment systems to speed delivery of HRA and FSA payments to providers. Soon you should be able to swipe your debit card and the provider of care will be paid the discounted amount without having to send you a balance bill.

IV. Copays, Deductibles & Coinsurance

Full coverage health plans are priced to minimize out of pocket expenses so that the cost of a visit to the doctor should not be a rationale for avoiding care. Since premium costs are fully tax deductible to a business, the historical tendency of employers has been to pay more upfront for the peace of mind knowing "the best coverage is available" to workers. Full coverage health plans eliminate barriers to seeking all the care a patient and their doctors think they need. Unfortunately over time, increasingly expensive premium rates emerge to pay for:

1. Utilization - Minimal personal cost responsibility too often translates to excessive and redundant health care use. Economic concerns are minimized in the spirit of available treatment and recovery.
2. Overhead - Think about it in terms of percentages. The insurance company / HMO adds 12% - 25% above projected claim expenses for administration processing, reserves, profit, commissions and taxes. Insurance companies make the most money from full coverage plans.
3. Provider charges – More office visits mean more revenue generated per patient.

Paying flat copays ($20, $40, $100) per health care service is a standard in most plan designs. Copays are convenient, although they mask the actual cost of health care services. **It is unusual in our free market economy to make a purchase without regard to its cost.** Well intentioned plan designers accomplished this standard for cost sharing with the introduction of HMO plans.

As health premium increases have outpaced inflation, advocates of cost efficiency have considered whether copays are the appropriate mechanism for cost sharing. Before HMOs, health plans included deductibles and coinsurance. Deductible levels increased over time and coinsurance responsibility averaged 20% of the cost of the care received, to an out-of-pocket limit.

Copayments generally replace coinsurance, simplifying out-of-pocket payment responsibility. Unfortunately copays also increase utilization of health care services, which ultimately increase premium rates. **Lower premiums result in plans designed to include deductibles and coinsurance, as cost awareness of each service is maximized.**

In addition, hospitals, doctors and pharmaceutical companies agree to reduce charges, resulting in discounts of 20% - 80% as payment in full. Reforming "charges" along with billing partial day hospital stays is inevitable with cost of service transparency. The automobile industry has had to adapt to this reality in recent years with increased awareness of vehicle wholesale cost vs. sales price.

The Medicare Part A deductible, which is adjusted annually, increased to $1,056 in 2009. To counter the low $135 Medicare Part B deductible, premiums for higher income earners have risen dramatically in recent years (Review the chart in Chapter XXIV).

The timing is right to assess coverage levels vs. out-of-pocket financial responsibility, since so many paychecks are reduced to pay a portion of health insurance premiums.

V. Prescriptions, Over-the-Counter Products & Therapies

The abbreviation "Rx" stands for the Latin word "recipere" and means "take, or to take." The English synonym is our word recipe. A prescription is an order to take a certain medicine. Medicines are compounds of various chemicals. Prescription Rx coverage receives tremendous focus because of the ever growing number of curative compounds available. There seem to be as many medicines to choose from as there are mutual funds! Prescription costs make up between 15% - 25% of health care premiums. Many medications are formulated for long term usage. A good allergy medication can, for example, really improve one's daily quality of life.

Certain medications should not be consumed with others medicines or supplements. Some medicines counteract side effects caused by other drugs. Drugs can be poisonous if taken in excess. Prescriptions are all "controlled substances" if they require a doctor's approval for purchase. This is because they are a concentrated mixture of chemicals that, ingested in very small amounts, affect one's body and health.

Dosages prescribed vary depending upon the condition of the patient, their age, body mass and gender. Often an originally prescribed dose may be reduced as a health condition improves. This question should be asked at every office visit by patients who ingest chronic care medications. Physicians and pharmacists may offer advice as to whether there are Over-The-Counter (OTC) products that will further improve their condition. Many 21st Century OTC products were at one time prescription medicines, and can be paid for pre-tax.

Frustration is common when the drug a doctor prescribes is expensive. High costs allow the developer to recover the research investment associated with developing the compound that results in a curative medicine. Patent protection for a prescription drug can last up to 20 years. Since at times patients believe they are overcharged for a controlled substance, it is important to ask if there are lower cost alternatives with the same effectiveness. Considering half doses to save money should only occur with physician approval.

The actual production cost of many medicines can be dramatically lower than their retail price, even if discounted. Distribution pricing schemes include selling medicines at a discount below the Average Wholesale Price (AWP). As a term, AWP is a misnomer. A drug must be significantly marked up to the Average Wholesale Price in order to sell it at AWP minus 15% - 70%. Prescription Benefit Managers (PBM) utilize this terminology along with acronyms like MAC (Maximum Allowable Cost) when establishing Rx prices. Like the charge master in a hospital, currently accepted pricing schemes are out of date and add to overall costs.

When Rx copayments remain flat for multiple years, a smaller percentage of the cost of a medicine is paid by patients. Awareness of the actual price of a drug prompts interest in value and consideration of alternatives. **Price awareness is one benefit of patients paying the full cost of a medicine versus a flat copayment.** This occurs in a qualified High Deductible Health Plan (HDHP), since prescriptions are subject to the upfront deductible.

Retailers who market generic prescriptions for copays of $4 to $9 per fill are acquiring medicines at the true wholesale, or acquisition cost. Low copays for generic drugs prompt store visits by patients to buy medicines, with the expectation that these shoppers will purchase other products while at the store.

Monthly pharmacy refills are inconvenient and more expensive for chronic care brand medications. Mail order Rx purchases reduces cost. Saving a monthly copay is the enticement to have three months of medicine delivered by mail. It is as safe as purchases from a retail pharmacy. Turn around to delivery averages 1.5 weeks.

Opportunities are emerging for prescriptions to be purchased through "overnight Rx vendors". This is how correctional facilities and long term care facilities purchase medicines for inmates and residents. Two day turnaround and Acquisition Cost pricing are part of this solution, with vendors including a shipping charge plus a flat filling fee to cover their expenses.

Emergency medications are becoming increasingly available for purchase at clinics and doctor's offices, assuming they are non-narcotic. This efficient purchase model is reducing reliance on short term medicine purchases at retail pharmacies. Most important to note is that it does not replace the value provided by well trained pharmacists.

VI. Why This is Covered and That is Not
Bev & Barry's Balance

It is a crazy existence being in your early 30's with four young children under the age of 10. Bev was tired every morning, even if the lights were out by 10:00 pm the previous night. The twin boys and their sister, who was only 11 months younger, had to be fed by 7:00 am in order to make the bus to school. Barry dropped them off at the corner on his way to work.

Bev had almost an hour after the older ones left to get the baby, now three years old, ready for day care. Drop off was at 8:30 am, fortunately right near her office.

She had been trying to shed the weight from bearing children, but it seemed impossible. Besides the cakes and cookies that were almost always available during the day at work, she did not like coffee and was used to drinking soda throughout the day to stay sharp. The sugar and caffeine combination was effective, though short term.

Her doctor had informed her about an increasing risk for diabetes if she did not lose about 30 pounds. It worried her, so when she tried dieting, it included switching to sugar free soda and a starvation ritual. Bev tried to walk for 20 minutes during her lunch break if the weather cooperated. This was the extent of her formal exercise routine.

Having the best health insurance was a major reason she had gone back to work. Since her parents both had cancer operations requiring hospitalization, she worried if heredity meant she was destined in the future to fight cancer. Barry worked for a large, national company that offered plan choices, but charged too much for family coverage. With her job, she could cover herself and the children for much lower payroll deductions. He covered just himself, and never seemed to get sick.

Always looking to save money, she decided it was worth the analysis to consider the new Upfront Deductible option, even though it included a $4,000 family deductible. She understood the HRA and FSA since these plans were offered by her husband's company. Most of their day care costs and medical copayments were already paid pre-tax.

Bev's chart of premium savings versus payment risk looked as follows:

Chart D - Bev & Barry's Financial Analysis

Current Plan:	$5,000 in payroll deductions
	<u>$1,500 in expected copays</u>
	$6,500 KNOWN COST
Additional risk:	$1,250 - $2,500 if hospitalized
Total:	**$7,750 - $9,000**

New Plan:	$3,000 in payroll deductions
	<u>$2,000 in deductibles</u>
	$5,000 KNOWN COST
Total:	**$5,000**
Additional risk:	Rx copays post deductible

| Potential savings: | $1,500 - $4,000 |

The premium savings supported making the switch, taking the HRA and deferring some more money into the FSA. Since the change was simply financial and did not impact their choice of providers, plus included 100% catastrophic protection for her and the children, it made sense. She also liked that it was one aggregate deductible for everyone except Barry. She wondered if at his next open enrollment, it might be worth his while to also switch.

What should we look for in a quality health insurance plan? It starts by confirming that hospitals, doctors and pharmacies allow geographical ease to receive services in network. Next consider the amount of freedom you desire when receiving medical care. Do you mind getting an approval to be covered for a visit with the heart specialist? If not, then an HMO with a referral system is fine.

Then, look at the lifetime maximum benefit, which should be at least $2,000,000. While you may have the stamina to survive the prodding discomfort of more than $2,000,000 in health care services, life extension without quality of life is a consideration. Many happy children are alive today who needed more than $1,000,000 to live beyond premature infancy. Realistically, quality of life usually drops significantly for individuals who continue to incur more than $100,000 per year in health care expenses. Plans that include a $5,000,000 lifetime maximum or are "unlimited" add to peace of mind.

Personal out-of-pocket cost responsibility is the core concept of this book; a subject with many points of view.

How much should you have to pay out of your pocket for medical care? Take into account health care deductions from your annual pay. Some individuals believe the best health insurance plan should result in no out-of-pocket cost to them if they receive health care services. Some health insurance plans are designed to simply cover catastrophic illnesses or accidents. These plans exist so that patients are not forced to sell their house and car if in need of care.

"Limited Medical Plans" and "Short Term Health Plans" that renew every six months have seen increased popularity in recent years because of low rates. Buyers should be aware they are not adequately insured for catastrophic and chronic care needs if purchasing one of these plans.

VII. Our "Wonderful" Health Care & Insurance System

Per Employee Average Health Insurance Premium

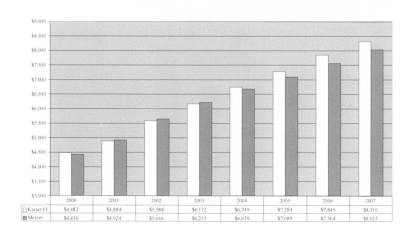

	2000	2001	2002	2003	2004	2005	2006	2007
☐ Kaiser FF	$4,482	$4,884	$5,588	$6,172	$6,749	$7,284	$7,845	$8,316
■ Mercer	$4,430	$4,924	$5,646	$6,215	$6,679	$7,089	$7,564	$8,025

Health care expenses are paid for by premiums, payroll deductions, and cash. American workers, starting in the 1930's were provided with low premium health plans, paid in full by employers. In the 1980's an increasing number of plans were replaced by lower out-of-pocket HMO, POS and PPO plans. Over time, premium costs for these plans increased at a rate greater than inflation, resulting in the introduction and ultimately the escalation of payroll deductions.

Insurance products evolve as a result of people's need and desire for financial protection.

Businesses pay premiums to maintain workforce efficiency, expecting that insurance will pay the bills as significant or catastrophic events occur. An efficient system balances coverage levels with affordable premiums. Employer interest in a healthy work force is based upon maximizing productivity.

The success of HMOs proves that health insurance coverage above and beyond protection for significant or catastrophic occurrences is desired by Americans. HMOs reduce payment and paperwork, pre-paying physicians for basic and preventive care services.

In the 1980's, one of the more popular health insurance plans in the Mid-Atlantic region was sold by The Guardian Life Insurance Company. This era preceded managed care, meaning there were not formal health care provider networks with the exception of regional Blue Cross and Blue Shield plans. Copayments for office visits and prescriptions did not exist.

The Guardian's popular health program was referred to as the "$100 deductible, 100% plan." It was simple and comprehensive. Some might ask why it wasn't simply a "100%" coverage plan. The answer lies in the relative value of $100 back then, plus the desire to limit premium increases. Using the consumer price index and moving forward a generation, the purchasing value of $100 in 1980 is similar to $1,000 in the first decade of the 21st century. Self insuring the first $1,000 reduces small claims activity, which lowers insurance company overhead expenses.

The Guardian product's popularity ultimately dwindled as the first $100 deductible barrier was eroded by inflation, rate increases, plus the loss of market share to copay based HMO, PPO and POS plans. Participants preferred $2 copays for office visits through a limited network of doctors, versus self insuring the first $100 of their health care costs.

The evolution of HMOs has impacted us all. This well intentioned concept effectively eliminated patient consideration for the cost of health care services. **The "numbing down" that occurred, where patients began to believe the office visit and the prescriptions only cost the $10 copay, has spurred retrospective plan designs now known as Consumer Driven Health Care Plans.**

In these plans, "transparency of actual cost" is the growing trend. Patients are financially motivated to learn actual cost of recommended health care services. With the passage of legislation in recent years, our government has approved new plan designs and health cost disclosure standards to promote this revolution. How much risk we accept when it comes to our health care is decided by one's employer, since they select the plans offered.

Phenomenal advancements in medicine are extending life spans, increasing quality of life standards, reducing discomfort and pain, and curing ailments. How much we pay, in comparison with what is covered by health insurance, balances insured risk and premium costs.

Most of us do not awake on a typical day anticipating using their health insurance for catastrophically expensive care. But the potential always exists. Changing plans promotes worry about lost benefits. We accept the paradigm that good coverage is expensive.

The list of diseases, conditions, treatments and therapies is ever growing. It is overwhelming and mind boggling. Terminology used to describe health problems adds to the confusion, along with our respect for its complexity with the years invested by doctors and other health care professionals to develop and maintain their expertise. If a loved one develops a unique health care need, we want the best care for them. Add the aches and pains of aging, fear of cancer, organ transplantation or premature birth, and the desire for excellent coverage is a top priority.

The cost of health insurance coverage depends upon personal circumstances. If you are an employee, your cost is the difference between the monthly premium charged by the HMO or insurance company, less the portion the employer pays on your behalf. Although averages exist, employers generally pay 50% to 100% of the monthly premium. They pay, on average 84% of the cost of single coverage, since insurance company rules require that at least 75% of the workforce participate in the plan. It has been consistent in recent years that employers offer to pay an average of 72% of the cost of covering family members.

A reality for many workers is that their employer doesn't offer them a choice of different health plans. This is often a surprise for the young professional that moves from a large to a small company. The health plan at small company is the business owner's preference. It is also the owner who decides how much to deduct from your pay for coverage. There are non-discrimination rules that allow for premium deductions to be paid pre-tax, which minimizes deductions and ensures one pays the same amount as other employees who are single, or with the same dependent status.

Tax law changes designed to reduce premium rate increases in the 21st century are gaining momentum. Upfront Deductible Plans provide 100% coverage for high cost, catastrophic care. They may be Qualified High Deductible Health Plans (QHDHP) designed so patients spend their own money for common health care services, including office visits and prescriptions. These payments may be made with tax deductible dollars through a Health Savings Account, or Flexible Spending Account. Since patients are responsible for deductible costs before the insurance kicks in, premiums are low.

When is enough of something too much? In our technologically progressive culture, this diabolical issue creeps into almost everything. Only after products and services are developed does awareness emerge regarding balance and efficiency. Enriched wheat flour, high fructose corn syrup and hydrogenated oils are great products, but they have their downside when it comes to potential weight gain. Sport Utility Vehicles (SUVs) are versatile, but burn more fuel than sedans.

For years, caring employers have paid most of their employees' health care expenses. The government eases this burden by making premiums a tax-deductible business expense. We have grown to expect ever increasing premiums, because of increased costs that pay the providers of care.

Health coverage should be comprehensive, protecting us like a warm wool blanket on a cold night, minimizing our exposure. Over time, how much we pay out-of-pocket versus how much the insurance company pays impacts how much care is consumed and therefore next year's premium rates. Many are concerned that the more financial responsibility we accept for our health care needs, the less care will be received. Judicious consumers will purchase what is needed, not just what is wanted. For defensive medicine reasons, at times doctors will suggest additional tests "just to be sure." Smart consumers learn to ask "is this test necessary now, or is this about convenience?" In the end, an educated decision is made.

Unfortunately, patients and physicians are disconnected from cost efficiencies when the insurance company is paying 100% of the bill. Without the checks and balances of personal out of pocket responsibility, premiums increase at their fastest pace due to increased utilization of available services. **Full coverage health care plans leave open the potential for "use abuse."** Often well intentioned, this tendency takes advantage of every possible test, procedure or product with the goal to maximizing knowledge about possible maladies. But does it always enhance our quality of life?

Acceptance of payment risk to offset premium increases is a growing reality. The concept of "health insurance," which includes payment risk, replaces a "health coverage" paradigm and becomes the emerging trend for efficient plan design and lower premium costs. Both approaches must include catastrophic insurance protection if hospitalized or chronically ill.

VIII. Contemporary Health Coverage Choices
Dave & Doris' Decision

Ann's boss Dave was very interested in the process she and Helen had gone through in concluding that the Upfront Deductible plan was the better choice. His family included his wife Doris and three school age children. Doris was in charge of dealing with the kid's medical care needs. She and Dave rarely discussed the insurance plan, except for getting certain prescriptions approved to treat the asthma of their youngest child. The copay for one medicine that came in a plastic disc was $50 per month, which seemed like a lot of money until they found out that its true cost was $145 per month.

Their current plan for the family was increasing in cost to $200 per pay, or $5,200 per year. Deductions for the Upfront Deductible plan were $120 per pay, or $3,120 per year, a savings of $2,080. **The deductible was $4,000 for the family, with the first $2,000 given to them by the employer either through an HRA or an HSA.**

Dave was not certain how much the family spent on copays, but he knew the asthma medicine alone cost $1,740 for the year, versus copays of $600. He and Doris sat at the kitchen table after dinner one night and figured out their current copay costs. The family used 6 maintenance medicines each month and averaged 12 office visit appointments. Since some of these were to treat sinus infections, the necessary antibiotics resulted in 3 additional prescriptions. With all the sports the children played, they could anticipate at least one emergency room visit per year including an x-ray.

Chart F - Dave & Doris' Financial Analysis

Current Plan:	$5,200 in payroll deductions
	<u>$1,350 in expected copays</u>
	$6,550 KNOWN COST
Additional risk:	$1,250 - $2,500 if hospitalized
Total:	**$7,800 - $9,050**
New Plan:	$3,120 in payroll deductions
	<u>$2,000 in deductibles</u>
	$5,120 KNOWN COST
Additional risk:	Rx copays post deductible
Total:	**$5,120**

Potential savings: $1,430 - $3,930

The family was likely to satisfy the higher deductible during a normal year, but they still saved money with the Upfront Deductible plan. If they put $2,000 in an FSA, this out-of-pocket cost could all be paid with pre-tax dollars.

SECTION TWO
Risk vs. Coverage Rationale

IX. It Really Does Cost Too Much
Amy's Analysis

Dave told his co-worker Amy, who reported to the big boss, that he was moving to the new plan. At first incredulous, she asked "You do well financially, why not buy the best?" He replied that saving for college tuition was a financial worry, so he was always open to new ideas. "By the way, that Upfront Deductible option may be best for you and your husband."

So Amy did the math. Although she had recovered from breast cancer three years ago, she remembered that there were few financial hassles, other than the cost of the copays. Now age 56, their macrobiotic cooking regimen had helped she and Jeff lose weight, plus eliminated the need for cholesterol and blood pressure medicine. He was 58 and had his own building and landscaping business. He loved the outdoors. Their children were grown up and out on their own; the first grandchild was due in three months.

Amy decided to heed Dave's advice and study the Upfront Deductible plan option. She learned that the deductible for Jeff and her was $4,000. Her payroll deductions dropped from $180 per pay ($4,680 per year), to $100 per pay, a savings of $2,080 per year. Dave had given her the worksheet from Ann's mother.

Chart G - Amy's Financial Analysis

Current Plan:	$4,680 in payroll deductions
	<u>$ 250 in expected copays</u>
	$4,930 KNOWN COST
Additional risk:	$1,250 - $2,500 if hospitalized
Total:	**$6,180 - $7,430**

New Plan:	$2,600 in payroll deductions
	<u>$0 in deductibles</u>
	$2,600 KNOWN COST
Additional risk:	$2,000 in deductibles
Total:	**$4,600**

Potential savings: $2,330 - $2,830

The interesting part about the HSA idea included the ability to deposit almost $6,000 tax free above the $2,000 provided by the employer into their own HSA bank account. Because unused HSA funds rollover, it offered them an opportunity to generate additional tax-free savings. Assuming they remained healthy, by the time Frank turned 65, they could have $50,000 more in retirement savings, in addition to the money in their 401k plan.

He liked that this new plan meant they no longer had to hassle with copayments. There was payment risk upfront because the HSA money accumulated per pay. Fortunately they had a significant reserve in their savings account, so if a costly health care bill occurred prior to building an HSA reserve, money was available to pay the $4,000 deductible.

They understood that hospitalization is expensive. Chronic care needs can be very costly, when you must return again and again for treatment, and pay a copayment each visit, as she did after her breast cancer. They both respected that certain medicines are available because of the investment by drug manufacturers and patent holder.

For the health care system to work efficiently, patients should not have outrageous out of pocket exposure for care needs. If people have to choose between spending money on food or medicine, the system is broken. This notion is often reviewed in news stories to reinforce that access to quality health care is a right. **The real question is what level of risk exposure is reasonable? Is $2,000 to $5,000 too much?**

The right health insurance plan should balance payroll deductions with one's ability to afford medical services. Financial efficiency is about thresholds; what we can and cannot afford to spend from our take-home pay and savings.

Take your own test by adding up what you and your family have spent for health care over the past five years. If the amount is significant and future expenses will continue to be high, a plan with low copays and high premiums may be best for you.

For many, an Upfront Deductible plan offers the opportunity to invest premium savings on a pre-tax basis that will become a safety net for the future.

Chart H – A Sample of the Financial Analysis

Your Calculations using Helen's Chart

Your Current Plan: $_____ in payroll deductions

$_____ in expected copays

$_____ KNOWN COST

Additional risk: $_____ if hospitalized

Total: $_____

New Plan: $_____ in payroll deductions

$_____ in deductibles

$_____ KNOWN COST

Additional risk: $_____ if hospitalized

Total: $_____

Potential savings: $_____

X. Alphabet Soup - FSA, HRA, HSA

A generation ago, FSA, HRA & HSA options did not exist. Back then, the touch tone telephone # & * functioned only in laboratories and at Disney World. There were no personal computers or Windows operating system, only screens emitting a green hue from basement computer labs. Typing had limited value in college but for aspiring writers and computer science students, since professors accepted handwritten papers for most assignments. A term paper or one's thesis could be typed by the professor's spouse for a few cents per word.

The 1970's was a progressive time and a bellwether period in employee benefits. ERISA became law in the first half of the decade, followed by today's popular triplets, Sections 401k, 403b and 125, included in the 1978 Revenue Act.

Even though a typical product or service that costs $100 today sold for less than $10 then, lawmakers were sensitive to the concept of tax advantaged personal options for retirement and health care expenses. Some employers were charging employees for health insurance coverage.

Section 125 regulated pre-tax payroll contribution standards, regulating tax deductibility for employee paid health insurance premiums.

Section 125 also validated a "flexible compensation" approach referred to as a Cafeteria Plan. Think about picking up a tray and choosing between the ham on rye and the turkey platter. Compare this to employees picking from a menu of benefit options including dental insurance and additional life insurance using financial "credits" provided by their employer. If one spent more than the allotted credit dollars, payroll deductions paid the difference.

Flexible Spending Accounts
Flexible Spending Accounts (FSA), a Section 125 benefit, allows the pre-tax payment of qualified health expenses as outlined in Section 213d of the Internal Revenue Code. In order to approve a tax exemption, policy makers included the acceptance of risk, known as the "use it or lose it" rule.

Until recently, FSAs have enjoyed limited interest because of this rule. Recent growth in the FSA has occurred due to the addition of a 2 ½ month claims filing extension, along with the ability to pay for many over the counter products and therapies pre-tax.

Enhancements in debit card technology that allow ease of payment for FSA purchases and the "uniform coverage" rule requiring employers to fund annual deferral amounts prior to full collection of FSA deferrals adds to the appeal of these accounts. A tax free, interest free "loan" is afforded participants that spend their annual FSA deferral early in the year. FSAs now also allow for the upfront payment of scheduled services such as orthodontia treatment.

At times the IRS requires substantiation (documentation) that FSA funds are used only for qualified Section 213d expenses. Follow up substantiation paperwork must be sent to the FSA administrator, generally within 30 days of purchase. If not provided, the debit card is cancelled and repayment demanded.

Auto-Substantiation is on the increase thanks to electronic approval of office visits & prescription copays. Enhancements to the Inventory Information Approval System (IIAS) also allows for electronic approvals.

Flexible Spending Accounts unfortunately though, do not "sizzle." With paychecks including multiple deductions, there is a certain leap of faith to appreciate Section 125 plan tax savings. The tax benefit shows up in your paycheck, because the Section 125 deduction is "above the line." So a $100 per pay deferral reduces one's paycheck by $70 on average. An excellent participation occurs when 30% - 50% of employees enroll in an FSA.

SECTION 125 & INCOME TAXES

♉ FIT (Federal)	18%
♉ FICA	7.65%
♉ State	3.35%
♉ Local	1%
Total	30%

$30 saved in taxes for every
$100 spent "pre-tax"
Employer FICA tax matching reduction of
$765 for every $10,000 deferred by participants

Sub S Corporation owners, directors and partners are not allowed to participate in FSAs. Discrimination rules requiring annual tests to confirm that highly compensated employees do not defer more than rank and file employees is another responsibility in managing FSAs. Pre tax deferrals for qualified dependent care may be offered as part of an FSA (through Section 129).

At year end, unused FSA amounts are considered "experience gains" and may be used to offset administrative expenses, or returned to employees in a reasonable and uniform basis. Employers usually cap the annual FSA deferral amount, usually at $2,000 to $5,000. Dependent care deferrals up to $5,000 are always allowed since access to these funds is limited to periodic deposits.

Limited and post-deductible FSAs may be offered in tandem with Health Savings Accounts. Limited FSAs allow pre-tax dental, vision and preventive care payments prior to satisfaction of the HSA deductible. A post deductible FSA allows pre-tax payment of qualified medical services once the HSA deductible has been satisfied. Limited FSAs are not a common benefit option, and lost their appeal with increased HSA deferral thresholds.

Health Reimbursement Arrangements
Average health insurance premiums have doubled since 1999 according to the Kaiser Family Foundation / Health Research and

Education Trust. Employers have reacted by limiting pay raises to cover growing insurance costs, and raising payroll contributions to fund ever increasing health care costs. Health Reimbursement Arrangements (HRA) allow a successful premium reduction option and have been available since 2002.

One must be initially "retrospective" to embrace the rationale for HRAs. A $100 deductible in 1983 had about the same buying power as a $1,000 deductible in 2008. Employers that implement higher deductible plans use an HRA to "back-fill" a portion of employee out-of-pocket exposure.

This approach reduces health care expenses in that:

1. Lower administration costs are charged by insurance companies and reduces premiums, since payment of first dollar claims is eliminated.
2. Use of higher cost products and services is reduced as awareness of value emerges.
3. A health care savings philosophy evolves.
4. There is a 15% - 75% loss ratio of the promised HRA benefit.

An HRA is an employer provided benefit plan that must be offered on a nondiscriminatory basis. Plan design limits are common, usually only covering in-network services subject to the deductible. The option to allow unused HRA funds to rollover to the next year is available.

"S" Corporation owners, directors and partners are not allowed to participate in an HRA. Discrimination rules apply, requiring annual tests to confirm that highly compensated employees do not receive excess amounts from the plan versus rank and file employees.

Health Savings Accounts
Introducing a federally qualified High Deductible Health Plan (HDHP) design, first available in 2004, allows for the establishment of a Health Savings Accounts (HSA).

A HDHP maximizes awareness of the cost of health care services, reducing discretionary utilization. Reduced utilization lowers claims costs, premiums and payroll contributions, thus increasing take home pay for plan participants.

The fundamental premise of a High Deductible Health Plan is to replace copayments with $1,200 - $5,000 annual deductibles (deductibles double for coverage that includes dependents). All diagnostic health care services are subject to the deductible, including office visits and prescriptions. Only preventive care services are paid in full, and not subject to the high deductible. If the deductible is satisfied, many of these plans cover 90% or 100% of additional medical expenses until the participant reaches a threshold, after which the plan pays the balance of health care services for the year at 100%. **All Federally Qualified High Deductible Health Plans include 100% coverage for catastrophic health care expenses.**

HDHPs allow participants the option of opening a Health Savings Account (HSA). This is a bank account owned by the individual participant. Deposits are not taxable as income. Money deposited into an HSA earns non-taxable interest and may be rolled over to future years. HSA account owners have the opportunity to build up pre-tax savings to offset future health care out-of-pocket costs. There are limits to the amount of money that may be deposited annually into an HSA. There is no cap on lifetime HSA savings.

HDHPs that allow the establishment of Health Savings Accounts (HSA), require government approved plan designs. **Since all covered services must be subject to the high deductible except preventive care, the full cost of sickness related office visits and prescriptions are subject to the high deductible.** Employers may deposit funds into an HSA to reduce employee out of pocket risk. The minimum deductible in 2009 is $1,150 for single coverage and $2,300 for family coverage. The same family deductible applies for an employee insuring one or more dependents.

To deposit into an HSA, an individual must be insured only by an HDHP. It is important to maintain the context that rules and restrictions regarding tax savings focus on Health Savings Account. Legally it is possible for an individual to be covered under an HDHP and a traditional health plan at the same time. If this is the case though, they may not make pre-tax deposits to an HSA.

Positives about Health Savings Accounts are striking:

1. Deposits are not taxed as income
2. HSA money is the property of the account owner
3. HSA accounts are portable, so a terminated employee keeps the money if changing jobs

New rules enhancing the flexibility and value of Health Savings Accounts commenced January 1, 2007. These rules increase the opportunity for HSA account owners to save money on a pre-tax basis for post retirement health care expenses. In addition:

A. Increased annual deposits to an HSA were allowed including a catch up provision for participants age 55 - 64.

B. Full tax deduction credit may be taken in a calendar year for HSA money deposited other than on January 1, assuming the participant maintains HDHP coverage for a continuous 12 months.

C. Employers may choose to deposit more money into an HSA for rank & file employees and less for highly compensated employees.

D. Individuals with IRAs may transfer money, once per lifetime, into an HSA. This will negate having to pay taxes in the future on the portion of IRA savings spent on qualified health expenses.

Money transferred to an HSA must be used for federally qualified health expenses (Section 213d), Managed Medicare premiums or Long Term Care premiums to avoid taxation.

HSA money is never taxed if used to pay for qualified health expenses. What is not spent in a year earns tax free interest and rolls over to the next year. HSA money allows the account holder to avoid income, interest and distribution taxation. Until age 65, if HSA deposits are used to pay for purchases other than qualified health expenses, the account owner is responsible to pay a 10% penalty along with income taxes. Post age 65, income taxes apply if HSA money is spent for other than qualified health expenses. Upon death, unspent HSA money is passed along to a chosen beneficiary, and follows the same tax treatment.

Chart J - Compares pre-tax health account considerations & options.

2009	FSA	HRA	HSA
First available	1978	2002	2004
Funding	Employee & Employer	Employer only	Employee & Employer
Plan Design	n/a	n/a	QHDHP
Maximum Deferral	$5,000 for Dep. Care	n/a	$1,150 S/ $2,300F $3,000 S/ $5,950F
Catch up option	n/a	n/a	$1,000 ages 55-64
Maximum Out of Pocket	n/a	n/a	$5,800 Single $11,600 Family
Office visits & Rx are Part of Deductible	n/a	Employer Decision	Yes
Rollover	2.5 months	Employer	Included
Interest accrual	n/a	Employer	Included
Portability	No	No	Yes
Taxation	Employee Pre-Tax	Employer Pre-Tax	Income plus 10% if not Sec. 213d
Section 213d expenses	Yes	Employer's Choice	Yes
Transfer $$	n/a	n/a	FSA & IRA
Discrimination Testing	Yes	Yes	Yes
Retiree Premiums & LTC	No	Yes	Yes, except Medicare wrap around plans
Loss Ratio	98%	15% - 80%	100%

S - Single; F - Family

XI. Copays for "High Volume, Low Cost" Services in an Upfront Deductible Plan

Today's health care consumers and providers are used to exchanging copays as the standard for payment. A flat amount, generally $10 to $50 is charged and collected at the end of an office visit or to complete a prescription purchase transaction. This payment approach is popular, efficient and easy to understand.

Rising health care expenses have prompted health insurers and HMOs to add $100 to $1,000 copays for higher cost services, including hospitalization, outpatient procedures, x-ray and laboratory services. These significant copays for higher cost health care services offset some of the charge for the service provided, without building awareness of the actual health care cost. Copays exacerbate the cost awareness problem, since often patients do not know or care to grasp the portion of the overall cost their copay represents.

CDHP advocates successfully lobbied the Federal government to approve qualified HDHP designs that subject all diagnostic health care services to deductibles, as discussed earlier. These plans allow participants to make pre-tax deposits into special bank accounts called a Health Savings Account (HSA). The tax advantages are great in that funds deposited and spent on qualified health care needs are not taxed as income.

For employees needing repetitive and reoccurring health care services, HDHPs seem more complicated than simply paying flat copays. In addition, the high deductible burden coupled with lower premiums may leave the impression that HDHPs are of lower quality.

An effective way to increase acceptance of Upfront Deductible plans is a hybrid design that allows patients to continue copays for office visits and prescriptions. These are low cost, high volume services. In addition to payment simplicity, there is a perceived value advantage.

Payment immediacy at time of service is preferred by patients and providers alike. Services subject to copays do not accrue toward the high deductible. This cost shifting means it takes longer to satisfy the high deductible. Properly designed copayments for high volume, low cost services should achieve 20% sharing of the total claims cost. A copay strategy in many HMO, POS

Chart K - Upfront *Deductible & Copays*	In NETWORK	Out of NETWORK
Benefits and Services	**Health Reimbursement** **$1,000 SINGLE / $2,000 FAMILY**	
Annual Deductible		
Individual	$2,000	$5,000
Family	$4,000	$10,000
After Deductible Plan Pays	100%	50%
Coinsurance limit		
Individual	$5,600	$10,000
Family	$11,200	$20,000
Lifetime Maximum	Unlimited	$500,000
Routine Mammography	100%, no Deductible	50%
Child immunizations	100%, no Deductible	50%
Routine Physical	$20 Copay 100%	50%
Routine GYN Exam	$20 Copay 100%	50%
Well Child Care	$20 Copay 100%	50%
Emergency Room	After Deductible, 100%	50%
Physician Office	$20 Copay 100%	50%
Specialist Office	$20 Copay 100%	50%
Chiropractic	$20 Copay 100%	50%
Inpatient Hospital	After Deductible, 100%	50%
Outpatient Hospital	After Deductible, 100%	50%
Maternity	After Deductible, 100%	50%
Surgery and Anesthesia	After Deductible, 100%	50%
Lab / X-Ray	After Deductible, 100%	50%
Physical Therapy	After Deductible, 100%	50%
Inpatient Psychiatric	After Deductible, 100%	50%
Outpatient Psychiatric	After Deductible, 100%	50%
Prescription Drugs	*Standard Prescription Copays*	
Retail Rx	$10 Generic / $30 Preferred / $50 NP	
Mail Order Rx	$20 Generic / $60 Preferred / $100 NP	

and PPO plans includes an "Evergreen" copay responsibility. If "Evergreen," there is no cap on the total amount a high frequency patient can pay out of pocket during a plan year.

An Upfront Deductible plan design that introduces high deductibles and coinsurance for low volume, high cost services, while maintaining standard copays for high volume, low cost services will reduce excess utilization and increased cost awareness. It also keeps payments simple for highly utilized health care services. These hybrid plans allow for the continuation of copays that have become the contemporary standard, thereby enhancing prescription therapy compliance, plan perception and ease of administration.

In order to make these changes more palatable, employers introducing this type of hybrid CDHP include a Health Reimbursement Arrangement (HRA) to offset a portion of the deductible. Utilization of HRAs averages 15% - 40% of the promised benefit when office visits and prescriptions are subject to copays. Copays do not qualify for HRA reimbursement.

The Upfront Deductible / Copay hybrid plan is well received by patients used to paying copays for office visits and prescriptions. Federal government approval of HDHPs that allow office visit and Rx copays will increase HSA savings for individuals looking to build savings for future retirement health care needs.

XII. Affordability – *How Often will I Use Insurance?*

Health care products and services relieve pain, neutralize symptoms and at times, especially in complex and sophisticated situations, are curative. The diagnosis and relief of chronic, painful and worrisome symptoms, especially for parents concerned for their children, is a priceless benefit. Health insurance is important so that if at some point in the future an employee or loved one becomes ill from a horrible disease or accident, the financial protection exists to cover the cost of treatment.

But what about paying the cost of treating life's discomforts? Certainly aches and pains exist that will not be affected by seeing the doctor. Evidence Based Medicine studies go so far to conclude that over half of health care services we receive are not clinically necessary. These studies have the benefit of hindsight since treating physicians cannot be certain of future outcomes. And yet there is excess care in the system, including the role of health care providers when they give emotional counseling, relieving patient concerns.

Unionized labor was a major factor in the founding of America's employer funded health care system.

Where our health care dollars are spent

ᘒ**65%** of costs treat unavoidable ailments, diseases & accidents

ᘒ**22%** of costs are for _**Elective Care**_ decisions including contemporary lifestyle treatments

ᘒ**13%** of costs result from _**Defensive Medicine**_ decisions by physicians & excessive care delivery

Wage controls to minimize inflation during World War II prompted bargaining for employer paid hospitalization benefits.

Now, only a few generations later, this laudable success is at the center of our ever increasing affordability problem. Little or no out-of-pocket cost to treat ailments is considered the gold standard for top quality coverage. The cost of health care services has risen more slowly than insurance premiums. An increase in the volume of services and procedures performed is a major factor adding to insurance premium growth.

This does not mean that people with 100% coverage are healthier. There have been times that well intentioned union leaders have bargained away maximum wage increases to maintain 100%

health insurance coverage for members. Since decision makers in most organizations, including business owners, are older than the average employee, the importance of 100% coverage is often greatest to them, or their spouses. (Younger members today will need more health care later, so fairness is not the issue.)

Watch Out!!!
Limited Medical Plans have grown in popularity because they provide coverage at a low cost, but they are misleading. Unfortunately they do not offer comprehensive insurance protection for chronic and catastrophic health care needs. These plans exemplify the adage that "you get what you pay for." This type of coverage is not designed to be true insurance. They are pre-payment plans with limits on the number of visits and prescriptions covered, along with annual maximums of $10,000 to $250,000 for hospitalization care. **Limited Medical Plans provide insufficient coverage to pay for chronic, catastrophic health care needs.** The same type of coverage limitations are often embedded into Student Health Plans sold through colleges and universities.

Short Term Health Plans providing coverage for up to six months are marketed by insurance companies to individuals between jobs. They include "pre-existing condition exclusions," meaning coverage will be denied if the insured person experienced symptoms, took medication for or had been treated for a health condition prior to the coverage effective date. Short term health insurance purchased for an additional six months, means being subjected to pre-existing condition exclusions all over again. These plans are another example that "you get what you pay for."

Student Health Plans often include coverage maximums and pre-existing condition exclusions like Limited and Short Term health plans.

*Chart M - Summarizes coverage levels
for employer plans.*

KAISER FAMILY FOUNDATION
& HEALTH RESEARCH AND
EDUCATIONAL TRUST

2008 Health Benefits Survey Summary
Of National Averages

- Payroll Contributions - Bi-weekly: $30 Single $140 Family

- Contributions as a % of Premiums: 16% Single 27% Family

- Employers Requiring Contributions: 80% Single,
  93% Family

- Deductible average: $560 PPO, $503 HMO, $752 POS,
  $1812 HDHP

- Hospitalization copays: $211 PPO, $223 HMO, $225 POS

- Office Visits, $19 Primary Copay; $26 Specialist Copay

- Rx Copay average: $10 Tier 1, $26 Tier 2,
  $46 Tier 3, $75 Tier 4

- Coinsurance out-of-pocket: $3,000 Single, $6,000 Family

- Average Monthly Premiums: $392 Single, $1,057 Family

- HRA Funds Available: $1,249 Single, $2,073 Family

- HSA Employer Deposits: $432 Single, $849 Family

- Composite Annual Premium: $8,758
  (averaged by the author)

XIII. The "Purchasing Health Care" Concept
Charlie's Choice

Americans have the freedom to make choices, including whether or not to be insured for health care needs. Some consider health insurance a luxury of our advanced society, while others see coverage as everyone's right and responsibility.

While financially inefficient for the cost of all office visits to be pre-paid by insurance premiums, the routine is established with the birth of a child. Scheduled visits to confirm growth progress are "pre-paid." Pediatricians chart growth patterns, administer immunizations and measure reactions. A healthy child experiences additional follow up care once teething infuriates the nasal passages. Nostril ooze that may or may not mean there is a bacterial or viral condition. Young parents run to see the doctor to be certain their baby is healthy and comfortable.

The pattern of "running" to the doctor has begun. Some children will first become exposed to viruses and bacterium while playing with toys in the waiting room. Prescriptions to fight these microbes necessitate follow up visits and more exposure.

As we age, decisions for elective health care procedures can lead to unexpected illness. The risk of infection should be a major consideration when deciding about a hip or knee replacement. Simple logic, like avoiding hospitals in the winter months reduces the potential for post operative infections. Recycled air exposure is a reality especially when the heat is on.

If we have limited or no consideration for the cost of a health care purchase, because it is paid in full by insurance or society, our sensibilities about return on investment may become skewed and lead to "use abuse." When knowledge about total cost is a factor, personal acceptance of the entire burden, both financial and physical will occur.

And then you have young guys like Charlie who believe they do not need health insurance. Why reduce their pay for protection when they rarely get sick? Clinics and hospitals can't turn you away, he thought. At age 25, accomplished in a variety of sports, he especially loved skiing and club soccer. No insurance was risky, but so was life. Charlie had declined health insurance coverage to have extra money for his sports adventures.

It was the story about a buddy who wiped out on his bike and hit a tree that shocked him into thinking about signing up for health insurance. Charlie's friend got banged up so badly that after two operations, including a titanium rod inserted into his femur, he was out of work for three months. His friend did not have health insurance and was now paying $300 per month for the next five years to pay off the cost of his care.

A plan that cost Charlie the fewest dollars had some appeal, should he ever crash, even if it meant one less ski adventure.

Chart N - Charlie's Financial Analysis

Current Plan:	$0 in payroll deductions
	<u>$0 in expected copays</u>
	$0 KNOWN COST
Additional risk:	EVERYTHING!
New Plan:	$780 in payroll deductions
	<u>$0 in expected copays</u>
	$780 KNOWN COST
Additional risk:	$1,000 if hospitalized
Total:	**$1,780**
Potential savings:	Peace of mind

XIV. Being a Health Care Consumer is Risky

Every day we accept risk. It may be physical, like speeding to work on the highway. It may be agreeing to a thirty year mortgage on a house. Paying attention to the total debt including interest payments is uncomfortably eye opening.

How much risk should one accept when covered by health insurance? It is a recent phenomenon that health insurance plans with $10,000 deductibles are available in certain states. Insurance for catastrophic care needs allows for low premiums, requiring the insured to have a substantial financial reserve if they need care.

Out of pocket payments are usually made after tax, while insurance payments are pre tax. Some simply do not want to hassle with paying the doctor themselves. With the advent of HMOs, most workers have not had to budget or plan for the risk of paying a large health care bill. It's more expensive, but it's easier.

Of course, with risk often comes reward. If only 11% of people are hospitalized each year, why do so many plans include 100% coverage for time spent in a hospital? We recognize that a hospital experience can result in hundreds of thousands of dollars in cost. It may seem counter intuitive to accept financial risk for such a circumstance, but it does make sense relative to the risk potential. Many shy away from this consideration by not grasping the concept of an out-of-pocket cap, where 90% or 80% in coverage transitions to 100% after expenses exceed a threshold.

And what if a certain service that enhanced your health is not covered by your plan? Was the positive result worth the risk of personal payment responsibility? Health plan mandates requiring that certain medical services be covered, like infertility treatment, is a blessing and a curse. Mandates increase premium costs for all to benefit a few. Instead of insuring against a potentially catastrophic expense, they inflame the sensibilities of some who question the merits of society having to bear their cost.

XV. The Need for Billing Reform

The importance of billing reform is not often reported, but should be included in reforming the American health care system. Insurance companies negotiate discounts that can equal as much as 80% of the "charge" for a medical supply or service. We must wait weeks following a medical procedure to learn its true discount cost. Providers hire collection agencies to demand payments from patients years after a service is incurred.

Price transparency is growing to increase awareness of the actual cost of health care services. Insurance companies, doctors and hospitals have defended the importance of keeping private the details of pricing agreements in the spirit of adhering to laws against monopolization and price collusion.

A laboratory bill for $400 can result in a $300 discount; $100 paid in full. The charge for a physician office visit may be $120 and the insurance company approves and covers $60 of the charge. Patients wonder and at times believe the laboratory and their physician are getting "ripped off." Inflating charges leading to higher and higher discounts becomes a proverbial shell game, similar in kind to the Oriental rug store offering a 50% discount every day of the year. Retailers will slash prices more than 50% only when going out of business, while high discount levels are used by insurers to showcase their "negotiating efficiency" versus competitors.

When charges for health care services are so much higher than the amount the provider agrees to accept as payment in full, patients end up confused, and employers end up struggling to confirm which insurer has negotiated the best discounts.

Our contorted payment approach benefits no one in the end, since services seem more expensive than reasonable. It also feeds a negative paradigm that prompts many patients to ignore bills from providers, increasing payment delinquency.

Recommendations for a single payer system conclude that dramatic change will reduce complexity and financial stress for many Americans. The end is clear, and Medicare reform offers a clue for resolving the matter.

With Medicare, providers must accept what Medicare covers as payment in full. Hospital representatives often state that Medicare pays less than their cost of doing business. Private insurance plans subsidize the difference.

Maintaining a "charge master," at times referred to as the "charges roster," is one of a health care provider's obligations. Medicare originally paid providers a discounted amount determined from the charge master. This payment approach was replaced in time by a flat fee system, but the obligation to maintain a charge master, or price list, continued in order to set discounts for private insurance plans, to charge the uninsured and for extended Medicare claims. Providers have the freedom to increase their charges without affecting the amount they collect from insurers.

A $160 charge for a $100 service equates to a 38% discount. Increase the charge to $175 while continuing to accept $100 and the discount jumps to 57%. **The Charge Master increases patient fear of the unknown, while accelerating costs for patients without insurance, and those who receive out-of-network care.**

Consider the insured patient approved for a 23 hour stay in a hospital concerned about being billed thousands of dollars out-of-pocket if he remains inpatient for a few hours beyond the period authorized by their insurer.

Conscientious consumers must be trained to be patient once they become patients because of contemporary billing and payment standards. **Fundamental reform means replacing the "charge master" with a more transparent pricing system. Allowing a maximum mark up (20% - 30%) above the cost of a health care service as determined by Medicare is just one idea to reform the current system.** An hourly rate system for hospital stays beyond approved insurance company timeframes is another opportunity.

XVI. Employer Case Studies: Upfront Deductible Plans

Employer savings on health care translates to lower payroll contributions, increasing take home pay for employees. A growing number of employers have achieved this end by successfully implementing Upfront Deductible plans with HRAs. The data confirms a flattening of health care costs for as long as four straight years, at a time of double digit health premium increases. This approach works regardless of the number of employees.

Employer A

A 15 employee construction company, in order to eliminate a 7% increase for their current plan, moved all employees to a $2,500 single and $5,000 family deductible plan. The employer agreed to reimburse the first 75% of the deductible using an HRA. At the end of the year, 55% of the available HRA funds were spent, translating to an overall cost reduction of 22%. The insurer increased rates for the high deductible plan by 4%. The company changed insurance companies and for the same coverage reduced rates by another 20%.

Employer B

A 70 employee advertising firm, in order to eliminate a 28% increase for their current plan, moved the employees to a $1,200 single and $2,400 family deductible plan. The employer agreed to reimburse 100% of the deductible through the HRA. At the end of the year, 75% of the available HRA funds were spent, translating to an overall cost reduction of 21%. Costs were 49% less than their old plan renewal premiums. Increasing deductibles while maintaining the 100% HRA reimbursement allowed for a second year cost increase of 3%.

Employer C

A 150 employee auto dealer, in order to eliminate a 14% increase for their current plans, offered a $1,500 single $3,000 family deductible plan, followed by 20% coinsurance (cost sharing) up to $1,000. The employer agreed to reimburse the first half of the deductible through an HRA, along with half of the coinsurance. Premium rates increased 11% the first year and dropped 6% for the next two years in a row, resulting in a reduction in payroll contributions each of the next two years.

Employer D

A 200 employee distribution business, in order to eliminate a 27% increase in 2004, moved employees to a $1,000 single and $2,000 family deductible, followed by 10% coinsurance to $1,000. The company reimbursed the first half of the deductible using an HRA and maintained copays for office visits and Rx. Premium and HRA expenses increased 3% the first year, fell 1% the following year, and fell 3% more the next year, after moving to a qualified HDHP. Employees experienced no increase to payroll deductions over a four year time period.

Employer E

A 600 employee social services employer, in order to eliminate a 32% increase for their current plan, moved the employees to a $1,000 single and $3,000 family deductible, then 10% coinsurance to $1,000 out of pocket. Rates increased 8%. The employer agreed to reimburse 50% of the deductible through an HRA. At the end of the year, 50% of the available HRA funds were spent, translating to a 21% savings over the old plan. The following year costs increased 4%. The next year the group experienced 0% rate change. Payroll contributions remained the same for three years.

Employer F

A 1,800 employee manufacturer replaced existing plans with two Upfront Deductible options. The employer agreed to reimburse 50% of the deductible for one plan through an HRA, and since it included a net lower out of pocket exposure and 10% coinsurance to $1,000, charged higher payroll contributions. The first year 65% of the employees selected the plan with the HRA benefit. Claim costs remained flat for three years.

XVII. Diseases, Syndromes, Chronic & Acute

Considerations about quality of life include rationalizing our fundamental health and well being. We all have something wrong with us. Diagnoses start early in life. Certain conditions will last a lifetime, like dry skin. Osgood-Schlatter disease sounds horrible; like Alzheimer's disease it is named for the person who isolated the condition. Unlike Alzheimer's, Osgood-Schlatter is a build up of calcium below the knee cap that is painful to the fast growing junior high school athlete.

Syndromes are multiple symptoms that characterize a disease or abnormality. Symptoms are abnormal circumstances, like a rash or a cough that may be indicators of a greater abnormality. Disease is a condition that impairs normal functioning. Chronic conditions are ongoing, like diabetes and Alzheimer's disease, while acute conditions occur rapidly and are intense. A broken bone and hypothermia are acute conditions. The common cold is a syndrome that transitions from being an acute to a chronic condition. It is also a short term disease.

Medicines that help to cure one ailment can result in additional conditions and side effects. Illness, injury, pain, disability and death are all part of the life experience. Science and technological advances in health care have improved living conditions for generations. We are a healthier culture today than one hundred years ago.

New diseases are named each year. Most of us are aware of the term "consumption." Many have died as a result of this malady. The term is no longer used today because science and medicine can so effectively pin point the cause for a health issue.

Unfortunately, diagnoses are not always accurate. Some can also negatively impact how we look at life and affect our hopes and dreams for the future. Mind over body stories are heart warming and can be awe inspiring. Many diseases result in short term discomfort. The aches and pains of life are part of the experience. Some are intense, some bearable and some at times self inflicted, like obesity or a hang over.

In the end, conditions like leukemia, a form of blood cancer, may be deadly. Many of the deadliest conditions are labeled as cancer, striking down people of all ages. Cancer is a disease, and because there are so many types and stages of the disease, some die quickly while others live a long time post diagnosis.

It is reality that all of us live with varying levels of discomfort. How we treat ourselves physically and emotionally offers the greatest impact on our quality of life. Even sick people smile, sending heart warming messages to the rest of us. A doctor's diagnosis, especially when delivered in the Latin form, might impact our sense of the future. A "Hypochondriac" is one of our best understood multi-syllabic words.

Medical schools hire individuals with chronic health concerns to train doctors in their bedside manner. The woman diagnosed in her twenties with fibroids in her uterus who can never have a baby enjoys a surprise pregnancy in her thirties. Maybe the original diagnosis was wrong, or her condition changed.

Curative health care treatment based upon scientific principles can be an inspired art form.

XVIII. Ask Your Doctor

How many doctor's office visits are diagnostic and curative? What percentage of the time is a trip to the doctor an "assurance" visit? Monitoring by physicians is an important aspect of providing care. They understand that the demand for health care services provided by physicians increases as more people become covered by insurance.

Do doctors want 100% of the care they provide to be paid by the HMO / insurance plan? Sit in a crowded primary care physician waiting room and consider how physicians transition from one patient to the next. They are not distracted by whether the patient or their health plan is paying the bill. Ultimately though they know that most of their cost of running their practice will be paid through HMOs and insurance plans.

Self pay is not common. It is often difficult to collect fees from patients who pay themselves. If self pay increases, the number of visits for the average patient declines. Logic follows that demand for services is a function of need and personal cost.

Our physicians spend almost every health care dollar since it is they who order tests, determine conditions and prescribe treatment solutions. Trusting them allows for the isolation of medical problems, their correction and cure. Physicians are often regarded as the brightest and most talented citizens in our communities.

Physician investments in training are expensive and last throughout their careers. Medical school debt can be so high that repayment schedules last as long as a home mortgage. It is an intellectually challenging and often uncomfortable career, especially for care givers assisting patients at the end of their lives.

Doctors must also be business people in order to thrive. They negotiate with families and hospital administrators, often working long hours in service to their patients. We expect these professionals to recommend solutions that maximize the quality of our health. We also expect them not to make errors.

America needs our physicians to help control the growth in health care expenses. We encumber them with malpractice insurance premiums in case of errors, promoting defensive medicine approaches. At times there is a fine line between malpractice and mal-occurrence. Reasonable non-economic award caps should become a national standard to protect against mistreatment, while at the same time limiting financial responsibility when the care, or lack there of harms patients.

As a culture, we should also constantly reconsider the financial value of our primary care doctors and specialists. Trends towards specialties should not be motivated by income expectations, as has emerged in the last 25 years.

SECTION THREE
The Big Picture

XIX. The Consumer Driven Health Care Solution

Robyn's Rationale

Amy told the big boss Robyn about why she was moving to the Upfront Deductible plan. When she explained that it all started with Ann and her mother Helen, you could see an expression of joy emerge on Robyn's face.

Robyn had learned about these new plans from a business owner who was part of a group that she met with each month to share opportunities and experiences. She was initially skeptical that this approach to reducing health care expenses would interest her employees, but the case studies were convincing. **In fact, the approach seemed to work well for all types of businesses and non-profit organizations. Robyn was frustrated that their current plan cost too much and that payroll contributions were sky high.** An Upfront Deductible plan with an HRA and i.e. FSA or HSA option seemed like a reasonable way to maintain quality health coverage and increase take-home pay.

The overall concept also fell in line with her mantra, "The 5 Ps," which stand for **"Prior**

Planning Promotes Positive Performance."
Ann's interest re-enforced the decision to give this
new approach a try.

It made sense to Robyn that insurance company
losses drop when the insurer does not pay claim
dollars until a $2,000 - $4,000 deductible is
satisfied. **She also agreed that exposing the
actual cost of health care services to her
employees might help them become part
of the solution to cost control over time.**
Offering to pay the first half of the deductible
made the plan more palatable; a 100% coverage
incentive up to a point.

The potential savings were appealing enough that
some of her management group had recommended
dropping the copay plan and only offering the
new plan. In the end, Robyn, her CFO and the
Vice President of Human Resources agreed that
such a step was too radical for their culture. They
figured that a hybrid Upfront Deductible plan that
maintained copays for office visits and Rx was a
likely transition for the next year.

Robyn also knew that she herself must enroll and
promote the new Upfront Deductible plan. The

tougher decision for her was whether to enroll in the HRA and FSA, or save money in the HSA. This was like offering three plan options, because the reasons to select an HSA were quite different from choosing the HRA.

With one child still in high school, and another in college, she and her former husband expected college tuition payments to continue for another six years. Robyn was only covering herself at this point, and had fortunately enjoyed good health, except for the back problem from an auto accident that knocked her to her knees every once in awhile.

She had been advised that most employers provide less money for an HSA than they promise in an HRA. In the end, the right decision was to offer the same amount for both HRA or HSA, minimizing confusion and helping promote the concept. Robyn's chart looked like Ann's.

Chart O - Robyn's Financial Analysis

Current Plan: $1,300 in payroll deductions
                        $ 420 in expected copays
                        $1,720 KNOWN COST
Additional risk: $1,250 if hospitalized
Total   **$2,970**

New Plan: $650 in payroll deductions
                        $0 in expected copays
                        $650 KNOWN COST
Additional risk: $1,000 if hospitalized
Total   **$1,650**

Potential savings: $1,070 - $1,320

At age 49, she could deposit $2,000 on top of the
$1,000 provided by the business into an HSA. She
also knew that she had the option to use the HSA
funds to pay pre-tax for all the same products
and services available in an FSA. Since she could
afford the potential cash flow risk of the HSA,
it made the most sense.

XX. Health & Wellness

It really does make a difference. Exercise and moderate consumption enhances quality of life and saves money on health care. Without French fries, candy and cookies though, life would be boring. Recognition and awareness of moderation and exercise techniques is a growing business because people need to change habits that have evolved from their upbringing.

Online Health Assessments, coupled with support steps to correct early onset medical conditions are an opportunity to maximize one's quality of life. Mammograms at age 40 and colonoscopies at age 50 are proven lifesavers. When employers invest in health & wellness programs it positively impacts the bottom line by increasing attendance and quality of output. The addition of Online Medical Records data is being promoted to enhance awareness of personal health factors while educating patients towards improved health. The hope is that these evolving tools reduce health care expenses and payroll contributions.

To keep cars and trucks running, periodic maintenance is a necessity. The same concept applies to personal health. Try visiting the onsite clinic at work, or take advantage of preventive exams covered by your health plan.

Re-occurring face to face wellness coaching at the worksite yields the greatest return on investment. This system of engagement becomes personal and assists not only the employee, but often their spouse and children. Promoting a combination of daily physical activity, moderation in food and alcohol consumption, no tobacco and periodic check ups, reduces health care "risk factors" and their expense. Good habits founded on a spiritual sense of faith and hope re-enforces quality of life, productivity and peace of mind.

High turnover employers are least likely to invest in worksite health and wellness programs. Personal acceptance of the need to monitor activity and food intake must evolve as a cultural expectation.

XXI. The Economics of Health Care

"Venture Capital Delivers $110 million for Advancing Spine Correction Therapies." "Hospital Drives Local Economy as the Largest Regional Employer." "The Average Senior Citizen will Spend $200,000 on Health Care Needs Post Retirement." "Pharmaceutical Companies Invest $300 million Developing a New Blockbuster Drug."

Headlines like these in our newspapers appear with some frequency. Newspaper writers and editors specialize in health related topics.

Health care is big business! As these expenditures grow, competition and price efficiency has not emerged with price fixing concerns, patent protection and the willingness by patients to pay more for health care. Should one assume that because a $1,000 procedure to reduce back pain is less expensive than the $10,000 alternative, it may not be as effective? It depends…

Our government collects so much in taxes earmarked for health care that it is our largest single payer for many hospitals. But the government does not purchase actual health care services. It is the physician community and each of us that purchase health care services. The government and insurance companies are the third party payer for what we purchase.

Even though complaints about services not being covered also make the headlines, complaints that healthcare is too expensive results from how much or little is covered. Government mandates to insurance companies are designed to be in our collective best interest. Government provided health care requires tax revenues to pay for the cost of services. Restraining tax increases as costs rise may increase waiting times and reduce availability of health care services; a fact in many countries.

Everyone desires the best health and immediate care when suffering. Affordability of great health care is one of the greatest challenges of our modern era. The Upfront Deductible concept with pre-tax programs like FSA, HRA and HSA may offer the best long term balance that allows quality health insurance.

XXII. Health Care Employment

Consider the largest employers in your community. Look at most lists and you will find hospitals at or near the top of the list. Hospitals always seem to be building a new wing or parking garage. Medical buildings fill up with physician practices in spite of a nursing shortage.

Economically, health care spending is important for providing all kinds of jobs. Colleges and universities benefit financially from training students to be future health care workers. Construction firms benefit from building new hospitals. Building suppliers benefit from providing the materials to build these facilities. And now all the new hospitals are constructed with private rooms to reduce infection rates!

This is big business. Demand for services will outpace supply until the aging baby boom generation passes on. Since baby boomers are living longer than their parents, a fall off in demand may not occur for another thirty years. Of course many people are living longer because they receive great health care.

Will we continue to invest greater resources in health care to promote job growth and overall quality of life? Let's get personal. What would you do if you knew a possible cure existed for you and it was only a matter of money to enhance your chance for full recovery? Obviously this is a rhetorical question to show why we will continue to see the business of health care grow. It is a good thing, unless our society declines in other ways because we devote excessive resources to health care.

The Role of the Government

Legislators and policy makers impact health care in this country by formulating laws that affect taxation of health care payments. The government also establishes payment levels for health care services. Government initiatives fund the advancement of our population's quality of health. It is a complex responsibility. The HMO Act of 1973 was approved at the end of the Nixon administration. It took ten years for the concept to become popular, but once accepted, health coverage changed for most Americans.

Today's reform goals for fixing our health care system include eliminating redundancies by improving electronic data systems that track utilization. What is not known is how much personal financial responsibility will emerge with reform. A concern exists that you might not have to pay much out-of-pocket for care, but you also may have to wait an extended period of time to be treated for chronic conditions, as is common in Great Britain and Canada.

The necessity to "wait for care" seems counter intuitive to our free market system. It is the author's hope that including the patient in financial decisions concerning their care and treatment will re-balance utilization levels. The time frame for a successful transition to increased efficiency will require formulating new laws and initiatives to change habits, including current health coverage standards.

XXIII. Medicare – When I'm 65

The terminology in Medicare is vexing. There are "Parts" in addition to "Plans." Seniors purchasing a Medigap plan (wraparound / supplement), plus prescription Rx coverage, end up with four types of coverage. Three of the four require premium payments. The option of purchasing one Medicare Advantage plan results in one or two premium payments, but if you travel extensively or have a second home in a different state, you may not be able to find a doctor or hospital that is in network.

It may seem complicated as you turn age 65, but like learning to dial ten telephone numbers versus seven, we get used to it over time.

Payroll taxes of 1.45% provide the funds for Medicare Part A. This program, started in 1965, insures age 65 and older retirees for the cost of hospitalization. Community hospitals often receive 50% or more of their revenue from Medicare Part A. Citizens who have worked and made payroll tax payments for less than 30 quarters (7 ½ years), when eligible, are required to pay $5,196 (CY 2009) for Medicare Part A. For those that have worked 30 – 39 quarters, the annual premium is $4,128. If you worked

40 or more quarters (10 years), no premiums are charged for Part A. Credit towards Part A is provided to married spouses of workers.

Medicare Part B is a voluntary program that covers the cost of physician services. Monthly premiums for this coverage are deducted from your Social Security check. The premium amount you pay depends upon your income two years ago. In 2009, seniors with the highest income experienced a 29% increase in premiums for Part B. Those with the lowest income experienced no increase at all.

If you continue to work full time at age 65 and older for a business with fewer than 20 employees, Medicare Parts A & B act as your primary insurance for hospitalization and physician services. If you work full-time for a larger employer, the company's plan is primary. It is not to your advantage financially to sign up for Medicare Part B until retirement in this circumstance.

Popular Medigap (wraparound / supplement) plans cover most of what is not paid by Medicare, including Medicare Part A & B deductibles and coinsurance. These "Plans" use a lettering system. There are set designs; Plans A though L. Plan C is

popular because of its comprehensive design.
In 2006, prescription Rx plans under Medicare
Part D became available for purchase. Part D Rx
plans are offered by private insurers, who must
offer policies that provide Creditable Coverage.
Insurers generally offer three plan options. The
least expensive Part D Rx plan provides the
minimum Creditable, or legal coverage amount.
**More expensive Part D Rx plans include
copays and may provide generic coverage
through the "Rx hole in the doughnut."**

The "Rx hole in the doughnut" is a brilliant
solution to the challenging insurance and coverage
conundrum. Medicare Part D is a phenomenal
success according to thirty million retirees age 65
and over. But it did not start out that way because
of its design complexity and fear of personal cost of
drugs in the "Rx hole in the doughnut."

Medicare Part A & B benefit levels are "lean"
as compared with private health plan coverage.
According to the 2008 Kaiser Family Foundation
/ HRET study, private plan PPO annual plan
deductibles average $461; HMO deductibles
average $401 (See Chart M). In addition, many
private plans limit how much patients can spend
out of their pocket, before they pay 100%.

This is not so with Medicare Parts A & B. In 2008, for the first time in its 40 year history, the Medicare Part A deductible exceeded $1,000 ($1,024), which equates to a 32% increase over the Calendar Year 2000 deductible of $776. The 2009 Medicare Part A deductible is $1,068. In addition, one hospitalization under Part A requires payments of $267 per day after 60 days in patient ($8,010), $534 per day from 90 – 150 days ($32,040), and then Part A government coverage is exhausted entirely.

Medicare Part B includes a $135 deductible in 2009, and then requires 20% coinsurance forever; never transitioning to 100% coverage for physician services and diagnostic tests. For this benefit, annual Part B premiums in 2009 are listed in Chart P.

Contemporary Medicare Advantage options include a Medicare Medical Savings Accounts (MSA) and Fee For Service (FFS) plans. All medical services are subject to an upfront deductible except preventive care under an MSA plan. Once the deductible is satisfied, these plans pay 100% of covered health care expenses. Money is provided to offset a portion of the upfront deductible. In 2009 there are plans available that provide $1,250 of MSA money to pay the first portion of a $2,700 deductible. Unused MSA funds roll over to the next plan year. Additional MSA funds are deposited annually.

Chart P - Compares Part B Premium cost relative to income.

Part B Premiums
2009

Incomes as reported on 2007 Income Tax Returns		Per Person Annual Premium	% increase over 2008
Filing as Single on Federal Tax Return	Filing Joint on Federal Tax Return		
$85,000 or less	$170,000 or less	$1,156.80	0%
$85,001 - $107, 000	$170,001 - $214,000	$1,618.80	10%
$107,001 - $160,000	$214,001 - $320,000	$2,312.40	20%
$160,001 - $213,000	$320,001 - $426,000	$3,006.00	25%
Above $213,000	Above $426,000	$3,699.60	29%
Married but Filing a Separate Federal Tax Return from Spouse			
$85,000 or less		$1,156.80	0%
$85,001 - $128,000		$3,006.00	25%
Above $128,000		$3,699.60	29%

These plans are similar to HDHPs for under age 65 individuals that allow an HSA. They are Fee for Service (FFS) by design, paying up to the Medicare approved amount and a good option for health seniors not able to conveniently access in-network providers.

It is easy to conclude when comparing Medicare Parts A & B, and plans that allow for Health Savings Accounts, that a "Medicare for All" system is a breeding ground for private, supplemental health insurance. Private plans will change in design with "Medicare for All," but like today's popular Medigap plans, current law requires individual insurance buyers to pay for premiums with after-tax dollars.

Passing laws in our great country involves compromise. A "Medicare for All" system may lead to reduced access to services, rationing of care for taxpayers, and a decrease in curative, technological investments. Questions arise as to whether the greater good will be served in this type of system, and whether citizens will embrace "one size fits all" government insurance coverage designed like Medicare.

XXIV. The Future is Now

Savvy employers are aware of trends in the workplace, whether related to salaries, bonuses or employee benefits. New options for health insurance plans are no exception, especially since health care coverage is a benefit highly valued by employees. With health care costs steadily rising, alternatives are now available that can minimize payroll deductions.

"Hospitalization Coverage" evolved as the first generic name for health insurance, and is still in use today. Medicare Part A covers hospitalization expenses, validating the term's contemporary place. With the addition of coverage for physician services, laboratory, x-ray, office visits and prescriptions, the terms "Indemnity Plan" emerged to describe hospitalization benefits and coverage of other services. "Traditional" coverage became the default term with the growth in popularity of "Managed Care," which includes Health Maintenance Organization (HMO) plans, Preferred Provider Organization (PPO) and Point of Service (POS) plans.

Enhancements to benefits tax law in recent years offers employees the ability to pay, with pre-tax dollars, qualified medical expenses through FSAs, HRAs, and HSAs (see Chapter X). Employers have a positive opportunity to drive costs down, as health care "waste" or redundancy is reduced. In order for this to work, these pre-tax accounts are married to health care plans with higher deductibles. Higher deductibles give consumers pause to truly evaluate the need of a health care service. The logic is self evident.

Often called Consumer Driven Health Plans (CDHP) or Upfront Deductible Plans, there are multiple variations on this theme. All of them utilize higher deductibles to affect patient health care purchase decisions, yet offer comprehensive catastrophic coverage protection if needed.

One design is the qualified High Deductible Health Plan (HDHP), where all services except preventive care are subject to the deductible. Even low cost, high volume services like office visits and prescriptions are subject to the deductible. Copays are part of these plans only after the deductible has been satisfied for the plan year (for a plan summary see page 13).

Another design has upfront deductibles for expensive, low volume services. Copays are charged for lower cost, high frequency physician office visits and prescriptions (for a plan summary see page 65).

The financial savings of these Upfront Deductible Plans have been astounding for both employers and employees alike and are resulting in:

A. Multi-year premium rate reductions
B. Lower employee payroll contributions
C. A reduction in taxable income
D. Rollover of unused funds to the next plan year
E. Simplified plan designs
F. Careful consideration of health care services
G. Reduced claims activity
H. 100% upfront coverage

So how does an employer introduce the concept of higher deductibles, while maintaining positive morale? For decades individuals recognized that their employer and the insurance company was "paying the entire health care bill." Now with the high premiums and ever increasing payroll contributions, they recognize a substantial financial responsibility even if healthy. Americans appreciate having control over their finances, and the freedom to make choices. As shown in

Ann's example (Chapter II) and Amy's analysis (Chapter IX), a paradigm shift emerges when an employee makes a "probable" budget of health care expenses (See the worksheet on page 50).

Financial savings with Upfront Deductible plans occurs due to the employee's careful analysis and utilization of health care services. Utilization is defined as the **quantity** of health care services purchased and performed. An upfront deductible gives employees a reason to question – not the doctor's diagnosis, but the testing or services that may be redundant or unnecessary.

In addition, paying health care expenses with pre-tax dollars, as well as the rollover feature empowers patient health care when making decisions. The ability to save those precious dollars for use on future, possibly elderly health care costs, promotes a lifetime savings versus spending mentality.

Let's review types of options that offer pre-tax savings.

Flexible Spending Accounts (FSA) have been available for 30 years. This voluntary benefit allows for the pre-tax payment of qualified health care products and services, saving participants an average of $30 in taxes for every $100 deposited. Deferrals do not rollover to the next year, which has limited interest in FSAs until recently. The ability to incur expenses over a 14 ½ month period has increased participation in FSAs, along with the option to purchase Over-The-Counter qualified products and services.

The Health Reimbursement Arrangement (HRA) was created in 2002. Employers establish a plan that allows for the reimbursement of qualified medical expenses, along with the opportunity to rollover unused funds. **HRA expenses must be entirely funded by the employer.** Depending upon the plan design and employee turnover, the HRA loss ratio will be 15% - 75% of the promised benefit. The expense to the business is based upon how much of the promised benefit is actually used.

Health Savings Accounts (HSA) first became available in January 2004, and are now in place for millions of Americans. HSAs require enrollment in a qualified High Deductible Health Plan (HDHP). HSA funds are the personal property of the employee. Unused funds rollover and are portable. **To encourage participation, an**

employer may agree to fund a portion of the HSA, assisting the employee to contribute on a pre-tax basis up to the annual maximum. Because HSAs are portable, the funding expense to the business is equal to 100% of the promised benefit.

The experience of employers C and D, described in Chapter XVI, exemplifies the positive impact Upfront Deductible plans can have on lower income wage earners. To offset 30% increases in premium rates in 2004, these businesses adopted "total replacement" Upfront Deductible Plans. Both groups budgeted a 10% increase in health costs in 2005. Due to favorable HRA utilization, they were able to maintain or reduce employee health care payroll deductions.

Employer F adopted their Upfront Deductible plan with an HRA as an option. It was a welcome surprise when 65% of the eligible workforce elected the plan. The plan merited the highest payroll contributions, and was chosen by the majority because they desired to be covered under the "best" plan available. Not only did the HRA reimburse for deductible expenses, but it also reimbursed the cost of office visit copays.

Concern exists regarding High Deductible affordability by the lower wage earner. The cost responsibility for one's health care needs must be properly balanced with housing, food and other necessities. Upfront Deductible Plans are not meant to expose patients to expenses they cannot meet, and yet reducing health care payroll deductions can significantly add to take-home pay.

Where do we go from here?

Business leaders accept the responsibility to educate themselves and their employees about contemporary health insurance options. The initial analysis by many insurance professionals about Upfront Deductible plans was that they involved too much change and were not worth the "hassle." This sensibility is changing as time has proven the merits of the approach, both short and longer term.

The major difference between Upfront Deductible Plans and Traditional Managed Care plans is that patients receive tax free reimbursements for most or all of their qualified medical expenses. These tax free payments occur through an HRA, FSA or HSA, and are evolving as the new standard for comprehensive health benefits plan design. The inclusion of a rollover feature and awareness of the importance to save for retiree health care needs is promoting a longer term view than worry about affording next year's health insurance rate increase.

Consumer Driven Health Plans and Upfront Deductible Plans prompt employees to make quality (not quantity) decisions about their medical needs, encouraging fiscal control over their health care expenses. In return, employer costs decline, payroll deductions may be reduced, and pre-tax savings maximized. These results are worth the effort of trying something new, as the rewards will be great for all.

BENEFITS GLOSSARY

Frequently Used Terms

ACQUISITION COST - The true wholesale cost for a health care product; what the provider or reseller pays to the manufacturer

BROKER - Professional representing buyers of insurance rather than insurers

CAFETERIA PLAN – Benefit plan that offers the choice between cash or one or more tax favored options

CHARGE MASTER – A retail price list for all products, services and procedures provided by hospitals and physicians. These prices are dramatically higher than discounted amounts paid by the government and insurance companies

CHIP – Children health insurance plans available from a state to state

COBRA – Federal law allowing for the continuation of health benefits post employment for 18 – 36 months, requiring beneficiaries to pay premiums

COINSURANCE – Plan provision where the insured and the plan share a percentage of the cost of services (80% plan & 20% employee)

COORDINATION OF BENEFITS (COB) – Plan provision designed to eliminate duplicate payments for the same service when an employee is covered under two plans

CONVERSION – Opportunity to purchase individual insurance upon termination from a group plan

COPAY – Flat dollar payments that are the responsibility of employees to pay a portion of the cost of a service ($20 / $40 / $60)

DEDUCTIBLE – Upfront out of pocket expenses that are the employees responsibility before the insurance plan pays for services ($250 / $500 / $1,000 / $2,000)

ELIGIBLITY PERIOD – The number of days post employment an individual must wait in order to obtain benefits coverage (90 days for example)

EVIDENCE BASED MEDICINE – A scientific method for assessing the risk and merits of health care treatments, or the lack of treatment

FIDUCIARY – Individual(s) who act in a capacity of trust and exercise discretionary authority over the management of an employee benefit plan

FLEXIBLE SPENDING ACCOUNT (FSA) – Employee per pay deferrals that allow the purchase of qualified health and dependent care services pre-tax

HEALTH MAINTENANCE ORGANIZATION (HMO) – A pre paid medical plan designed to limit access to specific providers for good health and minimized costs

HEALTH REIMBURSEMENT ARRANGEMENT (HRA) – An employer provided benefit designed to offset a portion of deductibles; allows a rollover of unused funds

HEALTH ASSESSMENT – A wellness program questionnaire designed to promote awareness of health risk factors, sometimes referred to as a Health Risk Assessment

HEALTH SAVINGS ACCOUNT (HSA) – Employee owned bank account allowing pre tax deposits to pay qualified health care expenses. Ability to make deposits requires enrollment in a qualified High Deductible Plan

HIPAA – Federal law passed in 1996 establishing privacy and non discrimination standards

MANAGED CARE – An approach to health cost containment popular in the late 20th and early 21st centuries

OUT-OF-POCKET – The employee personal cost for covered health expenses

PLAN DOCUMENT – ERISA qualified written description of plan coverage including employee rights

PLAN SPONSOR – The employer that establishes and maintains employee benefit plans

POINT OF SERVICE PLAN (POS) - A pre paid medical plan like an HMO that includes out of network coverage

PREFERRED PROVIDER ORGANIZATION (PPO) – A network of providers offering discounts on a fee for service basis, freedom of choice & out of network coverage

SELF INSURED – Benefit plans provided by employers who cover enough employees to pay for services as rendered, and maintain their own reserves

STOP LOSS INSURANCE – Employer purchased coverage to limit catastrophic claim exposure for a self insured medical plan

SSNRA – Social Security Normal Retirement Age that results in access to government provided benefits at age 67 for persons born in 1960 and later

SUMMARY PLAN DESCRIPTION (SPD) – Benefits booklet providing plan details

THIRD PARTY ADMINISTRATOR (TPA) – Specialized claims processor for self insured plans

UPFRONT DEDUCTIBLE PLAN – Health insurance coverage with low premiums and a high deductible to be satisfied prior to payments by an insurance company

USUAL, REASONABLE & CUSTOMARY – Prevailing charges from similar providers for health care services

ONLINE RESOURCES

1. US Internal Revenue Service on FSAs, HRAs & HSAs
   www.irs.gov/publications/p969/ar02.html

2. US Department Of Treasury on Health Reimbursement
   Arrangements   www.treas.gov/press/releases/po3204.htm

3. US Department Of Treasury on Health Savings Accounts
   www.ustreas.gov/offices/public-affairs/hsa/

4. US Center for Medicare & Medicaid Services   www.cms.hhs.gov/

5. International Foundation of Employee Benefit Plans
   www.ifebp.org/

6. International Society of Certified Employee Benefit Specialists
   www.iscebs.org/

7. Kaiser Family Foundation   www.kff.org

8. Mercer   www.mercer.com

9. Wellness Coaches   www.wellnesscoachesusa.com

10. Cardio Kinetics   www.cardiokinetics.com

11. Health Affairs   www.healthaffairs.org

12. Evidence Based Medicine   www.jamaevidence.com

13. DataPath   www.dpath.com

14. Relay Health   www.relayhealth.com

15. Vitality   www.vitality.com

16. Up to Date Health   www.uptodate.com

17. JP Warner Associates, Inc.   www.warnerbenefits.com

18. Warner Benefits, Inc.   www.warnerbenefits.net

19. Human Resource Administrators, Inc.
    www.hradministrators.com

20. "Making $ense of 21st Century Health Insurance Plans"   www.
    healthinsurancebook.net

CHARTS

Jonathan Pierpont Warner

No stranger to health care and health insurance, Jon has 25 years experience consulting employers and individuals on insurance options. He has also been a hospital patient five times in his life, most recently in 2007. Jon's wife is a cancer survivor and both of his parents died from acute illnesses while in their early 50's.

Born and raised in the Lehigh Valley, Pennsylvania, he is a graduate of Phillips Academy in Andover, Massachusetts, and Middlebury College in Middlebury, Vermont.

Jon is a Certified Employee Benefits Specialist Fellow, a graduate education program developed by The International Foundation of Employee Benefit Plans (IFEBP), the International Society of Certified Employee Benefits Specialists (ISCEBS), and the Wharton School of the University of Pennsylvania. He authored an article on HMO legislative changes that was published in 1989, and wrote a paper called "From Managed Care to Financed Care," published in 2002.

Jon's entrepreneurial career started after 12 years as a Benefits Consultant and Vice President for regional and national insurance firms. He owns JP Warner Associates, Inc. and Human Resource Administrators, Inc., a licensed, bonded Third Party Administrator (TPA). Jon is also a partner in Warner Benefits, Inc. with his brother Andrew. The combined businesses provide employee benefits consulting, insurance brokerage, claims administration, retirement planning and investment services.

Inspiration for this book emerged due to the long term value and cost efficiency results for every one of Jon's clients that has adopted upfront deductible plans with HRAs, FSAs and / or HSAs. Reigning in health insurance expenses using this creative approach allows the continuation of quality insurance benefits and is increasing take home pay for workers.

Married for 21 years, Jon and his wife are raising three great children. They live in suburban Philadelphia, PA. Jon is a dedicated volunteer at his church, along with acting as the Vice Chairman for the J. Wood Platt Caddie Scholarship Trust. He is also a trustee for the Philadelphia Boys Choir and Chorale, and sings in this internationally recognized group with his son.